Ibi Lepscky

Pablo Picasso

Illustrated by Paolo Cardoni
Translated by Howard Rodger MacLean

BARRON'S

First paperback edition published 1992
by Barron's Educational Series, Inc.

First English language edition published 1984
by Barron's Educational Series, Inc.

All inquiries should be addressed to:
Barron's Educational Series, Inc.
250 Wireless Boulevard
Hauppauge, NY 11788

International Standard Book No. 0-8120-5511-X (hardcover)
0-8120-1450-2 (paperback)

Library of Congress Catalog Card No. 84-347

Library of Congress Cataloging-in-Publication Data

Lepscky, Ibi.
 ₍Pablo Picasso. English₎
 Pablo Picasso / Ibi Lepscky; illustrated by
Paolo Cardoni; translated by Howard Rodger
MacLean. — 1st English language ed.

 p. cm. —(Famous people series)

 Cataloging based on CIP information.
 Translation from Italian.
 Summary: Describes the childhood of the
famous artist, a moody and imaginative boy
whose extraordinary talent was first recognized
by his father.
 ISBN 0-8120-5511-X (hardcover)
  0-8120-1450-2 (paperback)

 1. Picasso, Pablo, 1881–1973—Juvenile
literature. 2. Painters—France—Biography—
Juvenile literature. ₍1. Picasso, Pablo, 1881–1973.
2. Artists₎ I. Cardoni, Paolo, ill. II. Title. III.
Series.

₍ND553.P5L3813 1984₎   709'.2'4—dc19   84-347
      ₍B₎ ₍92₎   AACR 2 MARC

                AC

PRINTED IN HONG KONG

345 9927 9876543 (Paperback) (Hardcover) 345 9927 9876

Pablito was a moody little boy. His moods changed as suddenly as the weather. Sometimes he was sunny and cheerful and loving. Other times he was stormy and gloomy and bad-tempered. His mother loved him very much, but she didn't understand him.

One thing she especially didn't understand was his feeling about things. Pablito very carefully collected such things as dry leaves, seashells, pebbles, peach pits, and cherry stalks. But he ignored all the wonderful toys that had been given to him.

One day Pablito dropped and broke one of his seashells. Sad and angry, he threw a terrible temper tantrum.

"You have other shells that are exactly the same," his mother said, trying to comfort him.

But Pablito would not be comforted. He had discovered that things that seem the same really have tiny differences. One seashell is always different from every other seashell. One leaf is always different from every other leaf. One peach pit is never exactly the same as any other peach pit.

Young Pablito had discovered that nature never repeats itself. But he didn't feel like saying it. He kept it inside, only crying and shouting on the outside.

Afterward, Pablito went to his room. He started to kick his toys furiously. His mother didn't understand. Why would Pablito want to destroy his toys? But Pablito didn't really want to destroy anything. He only wanted to change the everyday reality of those toys into something else.

In Pablito's imagination, the wheels of his wagon were two big cat's eyes; the handles of his tricycle were the horns of a bull. If only he could remove them and put them on the head of his toy horse—what an interesting new creature he'd create!

No, Pablito's mother did not understand him. No one did.

Certainly the maid didn't understand one day when Pablito dipped into the tomato sauce and made funny scrawls on the kitchen wall. And, as if this weren't enough, he took a piece of charcoal and doodled all over a newly washed sheet. The angry maid had to work overtime to wash and clean up everything.

Then, two days later, Pablito's mother discovered he had done another strange thing. He had ruined one of the living room walls by scratching it with a nail. She had the sofa moved to hide what he had done.

She wondered if she should talk to Pablito's father. No, she decided. When he came home, he wanted to be left in peace. He wanted to relax, not hear stories about naughty children and angry maids. Pablito's father, in fact, spent all of his free time painting. In front of his easel with paint and brushes, he painted and painted and painted.

To have some peace of mind, his mother decided to send Pablito to kindergarten. She hoped it would help him. Perhaps, she thought, he will quiet down. Perhaps he will play with other children and learn nursery rhymes and sing little songs.

But Pablito didn't want to play with other children or learn nursery rhymes or sing little songs at kindergarten. And instead of drawing nice little flowers as his teacher wanted, Pablito furiously painted a big sun in the middle of a bright red sky.

"Pablito! The sky is *not* red! It's blue! Everyone knows that!" The teacher scolded him in front of all the other children. And the children laughed at him.

From that day on, Pablito didn't want to go to kindergarten.

"What will become of this child?" his mother asked with a sigh. "He's such a rebel! He's so hardheaded! Maybe he'll become a soldier. If he does, I'm sure he'll be a general!"

"But perhaps he'll change," the maid said hopefully. (She had just read about the lives of the saints.) "Perhaps he'll reform, become a priest, and maybe even the Pope!"

But one Sunday morning, while his mother was dressing for church, Pablito did something terrible.

He painted his little sister with an egg yolk, making her into a funny-looking clown! He painted two large round yellow spots on her cheeks, two yellow circles around her eyes, and a yellow spot on the end of her nose. He painted her hair in egg yolk streaks and her elegant rose-colored Sunday dress in egg yolk stripes.

His sister, in the beginning, accepted it all as a game. But when she looked at herself in the mirror and saw her yellow monster face and ruined Sunday dress, she burst into tears.

Her mother, as soon as she found out, started crying, too. She sobbed into a pretty lace handkerchief, and then she said, "Enough is enough! Pablito is going to hear from his father!"

His father was called and told about everything. When he saw what Pablito had done, he wanted to laugh. But seeing his wife and daughter's tears, he didn't.

Instead, he said to his wife, "Would you please give me my hat. And also Pablito's. We'll go for a walk. I'll try to understand why he behaves in this way."

They went to the beach. After a while, Pablito's father lay down on the sand and fell asleep. Pablito took off his shoes and ran barefoot on the sand, stopping every now and then to collect a shell.

When Pablito's father woke up, he saw on the wet sand in front of him something that left him breathless. Someone, with only one graceful line, had drawn a beautiful dolphin.

Pablito's father rubbed his eyes and got up to have a better look. But just then a wave rolled in and washed the dolphin away. Pablito ran by, not saying a word.

Going back home, Pablito's father couldn't forget that amazing drawing. Had he dreamt it? If not, who had drawn the wonderful dolphin? Pablito? Or someone else who had passed by while he was sleeping?

As soon as they were home, Pablito's father wanted to see what his son had scratched on the living room wall. He moved the sofa. He was astounded at what he saw. It looked like a drawing by a prehistoric man. It showed reindeer and bison running from men on horseback armed with bows and arrows.

Pablito's father then took the boy into his studio. He put a white canvas on the easel, gave Pablito brushes and an artist's palette, and asked him to paint.

Pablito, first of all, painted a portrait of his sister. And he painted her wonderfully, dressed in her rose-colored Sunday dress with ribbons in her hair. Obviously, he wanted to be forgiven for the egg yoke episode.

Then he painted trees, landscapes, horses. He painted lemons, doves, vases, and the moon.

His father was amazed. And now he understood. Pablito had an extraordinary talent for drawing and painting.

Lovingly, Pablito's father gave Pablito all his brushes, his box of paints, his easel, his palette, his canvases, his large white sheets of paper, his charcoal for doing sketches, his pencils and sketchbooks. From that day on, he stopped drawing and painting. He was happy just to admire and wonder at the great talent of his son.

When Pablito grew up, he continued to see the world in a special, imaginative way. And he shared what he saw in his many brilliant and exciting paintings. To the world, Pablito became known as Pablo Picasso, one of the greatest and most original artists of modern times.